Stevie Needs A Friend

An autism awareness series for kids!

Written by Steven Pereira

Copyright © 2017 Steven Pereira

All rights reserved.

ISBN-10: 0-692-87276-0

ISBN-13: 978-0-692-87276-5

DEDICATION

The doctor said "autism," and the horrific TV portrayal of kids wearing helmets banging their heads against the wall is what flashed through my mind.

Oh no! why us? The answer came back from the Lord, "why not you?" Everything in life has a reason. While emotionally we may not want to accept the things that impact our life in a negative way, we must continue none the less. We must press forward and not lose heart.

So instead of dedicating this book to my wife, mom or dad, I want to dedicate this book to every parent, and grandparent who has trouble understanding what has happened to their autistic child.

My prayer is that through reading this book it will help you to understand that while your child has a disadvantage in this life, it is our mission that you embrace them as if they were typical children and allow them to amaze you slowly.

I would also like to dedicate this book to all our special need educators and hospitals, who have devoted their lives to help improve the life skills of our very special children. I thank them with tears in my eyes and great gratitude in my heart for their hard work and patience in helping to mold our children into useful contributors to society.

Last but not least, I give thanks to my Lord and Savior Jesus Christ as without Him, I surely would have crumbled under the stress and financial burden of raising a special need child. My favorite bible verse that helped me through our experience is below for your edification:

2 Corinthians 9:8 (KJV)
"And God is able to make all grace abound toward you; that ye, always having all sufficiency in all things, may abound to every good work."

STEVEN PEREIRA

Why I wrote this book?

Autism now affects 1 in 110 children and 1 in 70 boys. Autism prevalence figures are growing. More children will be diagnosed with autism this year than with AIDS, diabetes & cancer combined. Autism is the fastest-growing serious developmental disability in the U.S. Autism costs the nation over $35 billion per year, a figure expected to significantly increase in the next decade. Autism receives less than 5% of the research funding of many less prevalent childhood diseases. Boys are four times more likely than girls to have autism. There is no medical detection or cure for autism as of 2013.

In 2003 a very special package was born into our lives. Our son Steven, who was a miracle birth. My wife conceived when doctors told us it was not possible. Then at 3 years old the enemy threw a monkey wrench into our world and our son was diagnosed with autism.

One of the problems with autism awareness or actually the lack of public awareness is the constant looks. My Son, who was 10 years old at the time has progressively improved, but some quirky behavior remains. To the untrained eye, it seems strange. But to those familiar with the symptoms, behaviors, and mannerisms, the behavior becomes a non-issue. But for these who don't, the strange glares begin. If you know and are aware of the symptoms, you'll know how to respond.

I remember being at a water park which is a super high stimulating event for him. Any water event drives him to a super excided state. Unfortunately, the intense simulation causes him to be impatient and he doesn't wait well in lines. So, he'll cut lines to achieve the event he wants! I was watching from a distance and as usual he was trying to work his way to the front of the line. An older man on line with his kids was tapping my son and hollering at him to get to the back of the line. I quickly ran to rescue him. I removed his hand from my Son and politely informed him that my son struggles with autism. The man didn't know what to say.

Not too long after that incident, I wrote this poem and I would like to share it with you....

STEVIE NEEDS A FRIEND

Don't Look at My Kid

Autism Awareness Poem by Pastor Steven Pereira 8/30/2013

When they look at you and close their eyes....
don't look at my kid.

When they seem too old to hold daddy's hand....
don't look at my kid.

When they jump around and flap their hands....
don't look at my kid.

When they give you an answer that you don't understand....
don't look at my kid.

When they mutter and giggle and jump up and down....
don't look at my kid.

If you're thinking they're strange but you haven't a clue.....
don't look at my kid.

If you see them crying when you don't think that they should...
don't look at my kid.

If you think they're retarded, then shame on you...
don't look at my kid.

If they seem too old to be kissing their daddy's cheek then....
don't look at my kid.

If they're erratic behavior is bothering you then....
don't look at my kid.

If you know nothing of autism, you won't know what to do...
don't look at my kid.

Families with autism struggle each day.

Broken spirits for what their child goes through, haunts them each day.

Hurting hearts and pocket books too.

STEVEN PEREIRA

In God's hands we commit them each day, not knowing what will happen or what they will do, or say.

We live by faith with them day by day, not sure how will they fair in life, when we pass away.

So next time you see us don't look away. Turn your judgmental frown the other way!

Smile and say hi and have a Blessed Day! Then look at my kid and pray for a cure and that God would heal them before we are through.

See past the silence and look at their hearts. See past the behavior that you may not like.

Be grateful to God that it's not you, our kids are truly special and have feelings too.

AKNOWLEDGMENTS

I would like to acknowledge Maria Salas for her creativity and vision for Stevie's character rendition. Thank you for your patience in this project in dealing with me and all my questions. God bless you!

STEVEN PEREIRA

A Child was born to a mommy and daddy. The stork huffed and puffed.

"A baby was promised and I'll deliver him today!" He flew strong and brave through the wind that day.

When their baby arrived this made them so very, very happy. Daddy shouted with glee! "I'll name my boy Stevie because he looks just like me!"

Mommy just laughed and said, "fine by me." They whisked their boy home in jubilee.

Stevie grew, grew, and grew and started talking just like you and just like me.

Vroom! Vroom goes the truck. Some haul dirt and some pick it up.

But then one day, when Stevie turned three, he just stopped talking, oh so suddenly.

And when mommy and daddy looked his way, he'd turn his head the other way.

This made mommy and daddy very, very, sad. So off to the doctor's office they did dash.

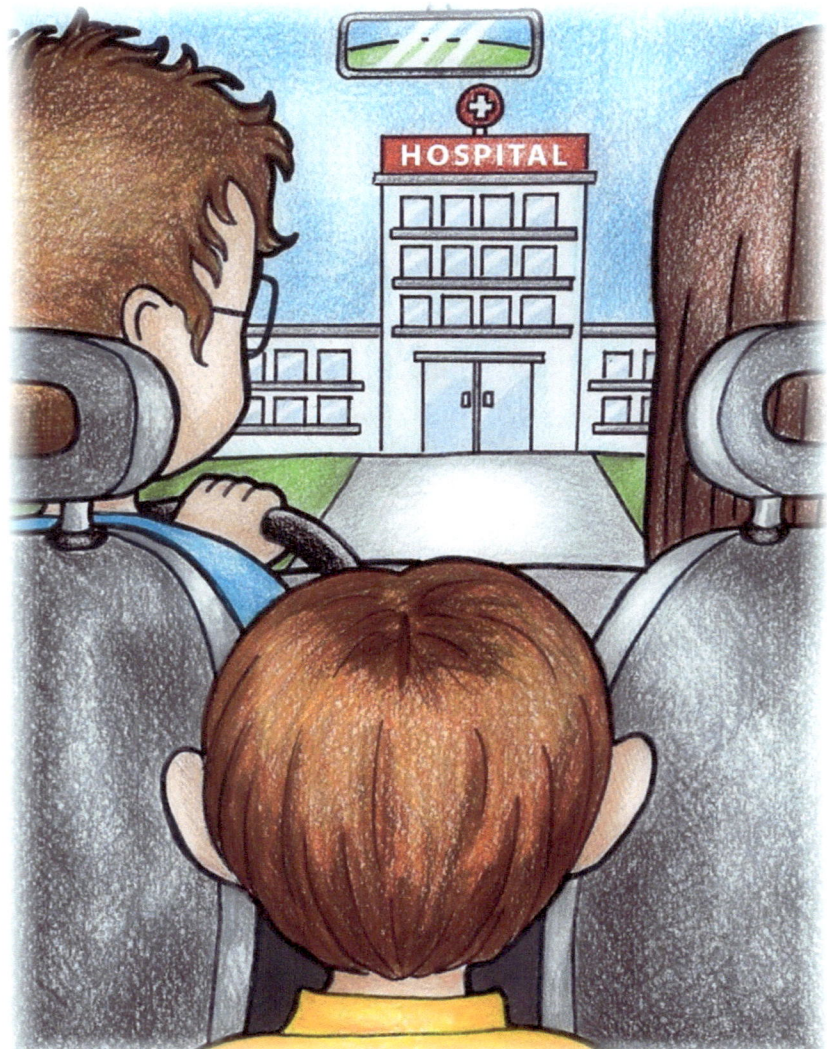

The doctor checked him from head to toe and said "Stevie may be autistic, you know. So off to the Special Hospital he must go.

Your boy may be different and not do many things."

This made mommy and daddy sad inside, this autism seemed bad in this moment and time, but soon they would see a much brighter side.

Later that night Stevie's mommy and daddy prayed. That God would help them along the way.

That night God gave them comfort and peace. They held hands with each other as they fell asleep.

The people at the hospital were really great!

They said "Do not be afraid. Do not fear, your little Stevie will win this fight, and do real well in this life!"

Stevie may not speak much, his words are few. But he speaks with his body like you and like me.

He points here, he points there. He looks here, there, and everywhere!

So pay attention as to where he looks.

Watch his feet, they will lead the way, then you will know where he wants to play!

Autistic kids are just like me and you, they want to play that is very true.

Just because he acts different, don't count him out. He can walk in a circle, jump and shout!

It's why they need good friends like you!

Someone to show them what to do, because their mind is being blocked as to what to think, say and do.

What seems easy to you and me, is like building a castle from jelly you see.

Stevie's mind is not like yours or mine, here's what's going on inside.

If you speak too fast, he may not understand. Around his mind they go!

Like a race car flying around the track, it's hard for him to get the words right back.

If you ask too many questions one after another, the idea of your questions is like squeezing butter.

They slip through his mind, they get mixed and squished. Like food in a blender, the words go whoosh!

When this thing called autism clouds his mind, he gets upset and sometimes cries.

Don't think he is mad when he doesn't answer or walks away. He needs help with an answer, just tell him what to say!

How can I Say it? Understand this, if a kid has a cast on their arm and leg, you can't expect them to play in a basketball game?

And so, with autism this is true, their minds are much different, but they love fun too!

Stevie can run, run, run around the playground all day.

His favorite is high up on the swing all day. The higher the faster he'll do in a breeze. He feels like the man on the flying trapeze!

Stevie can swim round about in a pool all day.

He'll swim, swim, swim until you tell him to stop, or to take a break to drink soda pop.

If he goes swimming in a pond or a lake, even the fish get tired of his swimming all day!

Splash, splash, splash his arms go! When will he stop? Nobody knows!

With help from the hospital and his school, Stevie can speak better than in the beginning, when this thing called autism kept his head spinning.

A,b,c,d,1, 2, 3, look he is learning like you and like me!

Now he can say "thank you" and "Please,"
he says "I need the bathroom,"
and "Help me please!"

Mommy smiles each time he speaks, proud that he has learned these things.

He's learning to speak each passing day, with help from others to show the way.

To some, special needs kids seem like a bother, not knowing that they would be a friend like no other!

Kids with autism are people too. They want to learn to read and write, many of them are very bright.

So before you frown because he's breaking rules, understand he knows not what to do. What's easy for you he can't comprehend, so consider an autistic kid as a friend?

Loving an autistic child is the key of helping them through this life you see.

Because without you they will never know, the joy of having a friend like you! To teach them the words and games to play and to help them to learn along the way.

THE END

ABOUT THE AUTHOR

Steven Pereira is the lead Pastor and founder of Together with Christ Church in Toms River, NJ. He is married to his best friend Cindy and they have an autistic son, Steven Jr.

"Stevie Needs a Friend," is the first release of a series of children's books to help raise awareness and to encourage exchange between autistic and typical children.

In 2012, Rev. Steven also published a title called, "Letters of Grace – A true life devotional." It is available at amazon.com.

Born and raised in Bronx, Steven hustled in the streets of city life, struggling with drugs and alcohol. Then 1994 he was introduced to Jesus Christ and He cleansed him from the inside out.

In 2002 the Lord called him to attend bible college, so they sold all they had and moved to Broken Arrow, Oklahoma to attend "Rhema Bible College." He graduated with a 4.0 GPA and founded Steven Pereira Ministries dba Together With Christ Church in 2012. (website: www.twccnj.org).

"Writing has always been an outlet for me and I believe The Lord is moving me to do more of it. I hope to continue my writing career as The Lord directs me."

We would love your feed-back on this book. You can e-mail us at pastorsteventwcc@gmail.com.

www.ingramcontent.com/pod-product-compliance
Lightning Source LLC
Chambersburg PA
CBHW042116040426
42449CB00002B/68